poems about love and space stuff
and some other subjects

by storey campbell

*for Grandma Jean.
I miss you.*

*for my dad.
thank you for never
giving up.*

*for Matias.
See you soon.*

*for Ori.
I took a stab at it.
is that joke still funny?*

*for Sam and Cherylin
when's our next D&D game?*

Contents

Without a Name 5

ants. 5

Breathe 6

water 6

Reflection 7

The Spectrum 8

Broken Clocks and Stardust 9

A Goodbye Letter 11

we'll do better next time 13

hey, do me a favor? 15

17 17

My Steps for Living Through a Day 18

the rest of my life: A Story of Unrequited Love 20

What MapQuest Says When You Put Me In as the Destination 22

Love Letter 25

The Man Who Brings Cold Wherever He Goes 27

She, The Ideal Me 29

Brass 30

Brass II 32

An Untitled Collection of Short Poems 34

Seeds of Saturn 36

Without a Name

Take me to a place
with our own name
where nothing is set in stone
where our pencils hit the paper
and we can feel so pleasantly alone.

Let me take you somewhere
my friend
where we write in the stone
to keep things true
though truly, my friend
we are in this place already.
As our pencils are made from stone
Itself.

ants.

There are these
little ants
with little voices
Crawling in my head
through my ears

They say these
horrible horrible
things
and I wish that they
would just go away

Breathe

All this air around me is filled with poison
Many who come near find it very difficult to breathe
More often than not, in fact,
they find it much easier to leave.

When you've got an atmosphere like mine, you see
You find out very quickly
That the best way to overcome the
Suffocation, asphyxiation
of living in the world that we do
Is to just stop breathing.

water

I am surrounded B
y water so thick
that Time gets stuck in
the Thickness
of the water
I am surrounded By
Time

Reflection

A dead person's face sits displayed upon my computer screen.
And with their dead eyes and their dead mouth and their
dead fucking face the dead person just sits
displayed upon my computer screen.

One problem with your perception of
the dead person with a dead face and dead eyes
displayed upon my computer screen
is that my computer screen is an unpowered void of blackness.
And there are no pixels
upon my computer screen at this current moment of time
to display the dead person with their dead face and dead mouth
and their dead eyes
which makes this dead person a simple [title]
of the person staring at the computer screen
which makes this dead person a simple grouping of
photons and protons and particles
punching my eyes like the waves of a slow-rolling river.

The dead person with their dead face and dead eyes
that sits displayed upon my screen
their bones are not always going to be
their bones will not always be
their bones are not their bones
For my bones are not mine and
friend, your bones are not yours.

The Spectrum

There is a spectrum
upon which
Everything lies.

Yeah, I said it!
It makes stuff up.
Everything lies.

The you that you see
is not the same you
that me sees.

And I hope the me that
you sees is not the me
that me sees
you see because Everything lies
upon a Spectrum
and as far as I am concerned
I lie pretty low
on the Spectrum

But then again
Everything lies.

Broken Clocks and Stardust

One of the things that sets clocks apart from other breakable things is that, when they break, you can tell the exact
    moment they broke. Down to the second.
I'd love to be stardust someday.
I think that people are often the same way. If someone is telling you their truth, as one only could, it's not hard to see the
    exact moment that they broke.
To be a nebulous mass of gas and ice and pressure and light-bending black holes because even then I fear that I might be
    suicidal and tearing myself apart from the core.

Now, unfortunately, humans can break over and over again. That's sort of where my clock analogy breaks down. Hmph.
I think, no, I know that I was stardust, a long time ago. I don't think I was a person between then and now, and maybe
    that explains my anxiety, I've not had any time or tries to prepare for humanhood like the others.
I know I've written about you before, but that time we were driving home through that storm of water and emotion after
    we'd all become broken clocks again, that was what hit me with that realization.
You remind me of stardust. You, with the laugh so vibrant and oh god this isn't the right poem to gush in.
I think, no, I know that my particular bit of stardust was chaotic, with great bolts of lightning arcing from cloud to cloud,
    it was like that storm and, oh god, why does everything always lead back to you?
And, oh god, that laugh could play me like an instrument.

Now, depression, which is one of the things that has made me a broken clock on many an occasion is often misconstrued
    as a something.
One of the most satisfying parts of the idea of being a nebula is the fact that I would be, likely, the only thing to break up
    the endless void of space. I would be something where otherwise there is nothing to overwhelm or hurt or

Depression is not something. It is not a cloud which envelopes you, nor a dog which follows you, nor some other
    justification for romanticization of the endless void which exists deep inside where my personality should be.
I could be something, in the void. I could be *the* something. And maybe, just maybe, I could help someone else with a
    problem of voids. If they could find my great chaos and bright purple gases and lightning in their   soundless void
    of space I could help them to realize that no, my friend, your void is not empty.
Depression is a lack of anything. It is emptiness. It is no emotion, no energy, no desire to continue to push for life to keep
    on going. It is sobbing into the pillow because, oh god, it hurts so bad to keep moving and thinking and being just
    because of this emptiness of anything inside. Maybe if I keep on searching I'll find some stardust in there. If only
    it didn't hurt so bad.
Now, I know I said I wouldn't talk about you again but, oh god, I really hope that when I am stardust. And you are
    stardust.
That what is between us is not void, it is not empty, no, it is not a cloud of darkness which envelopes nor a dog which
    follows.
I hope we can be stardust together.

A Goodbye Letter

You're still on my mind.
A lot has changed, since you left. I miss you.
I wanted to write
you another letter. I wanted to tell you
where the other letters that I've written to
you have gone. and where they
Are.

We need to start our journey on the
first layer of my existence.
It is not a very helpful place
to itself.
The First Layer
is a forest. Heavily wooded, and whose
tree's canopies darken everything
Around. Many lose their way in the
first layer.

Even though my heart is now beating as though
I have run far too many miles for my
poor atrophied muscles
The second layer is slow. It is a trudge
through snow
twelve feet high. In
The Second Layer
thoughts slow, freeze
to a stop and only the strongest thoughts
may dig their way back to the surface of the
second layer.

Our journey means to finish here
but I am unsure if it will end here.
the third layer is a beach upon a
Great and Infinite Ocean.
Upon the beach, my friend,
I have written you
and the others I have lost

into many letters, like this one,
and folded you into paper boats.
Upon the beach there is a bench
and upon the bench I sit and watch as you
and the others I have lost
sink into the depths of my
Great and Infinite Ocean.

I could stop here and let you wonder
what the final layer of this journey would be.
but that would not do this letter any justice.
No, you see, the innermost layer of my existence
is a sun.
It is an enormous giant, a hot ball of gas
in front of which I am constantly exposed to the
solar radiation of a thousand degrees of fire.

Exposure to the radiation causes my nails to curl   and crumble
and clink into my pockets like loose change
and then comes the hair
It falls from my body like a landslide from a mountain.
Later burns away the flesh from my bones
until I am not but bones wired together by the stress it would feel
to fall apart again.
Until I am a skeleton.
I am a skeleton.
Now, you know why you've remained
for so long. Because until now
your boat hasn't sunk yet. The letter in which
I had written you and then the boat in which
I have folded you
did not take on water. It did not sog nor
crumble below the weight and until now
your boat hadn't sunk.
And now it has. And so,
this is goodbye.

we'll do better next time

I stand before the great beast
clad in armor, scuffed from many endless blows on the field
of battle. This armor is not like most - it is not
smithed from metal or the leather of animals,
my armor is made from memories.
It is weaved with wisdom
restored with resolve
and studded with strength.

The creature has taken the form of
a serpent, this time.
It has chosen the name Basilisk,
to match its form,
and because the word begins mundane and quickly becomes harsh
as that is the nature of the beast.
"Back here again, are we?" roars the basilisk,
"You do remember this is all in your head?"

"I remember, Basilisk." I reply. It hisses with self-absorbed contentment
upon hearing me utter its name.
"How many times have we met, now?" I ask it, and sit cross legged, as is our ritual.
"Too many times to count." Replies the beast, with a voice almost seductive.
"And this time, you will not be leaving alive."
"Why must we do this every time, Basilisk?" I ask, as is customary between us.

Voice like daggers
the basilisk says, "Because I hate you."
"Because you are pathetic," it spits.
"I will bear down upon you like the sun over the desert, like gravity over the earth
I will devour your memories
And I will corrupt your wisdom

and I will break your resolve
And it is because of me, Basilisk, that you will die."

By now, the beast had grown to twice its previous size, and its mouth dripped
saliva and venom all around me.
"No." I say. I stand, and stare the beast in its monstrous eyes.
"No, beast. Like every time before, you will not succeed. Because without me, there is no you.
You depend on me, you are as much a part of me as my muse or my left hand,
And for that, I will love you.
I will love you like a 90 mile per hour collision loves the bodies in the cars
I will love you because despite everything I am you and you are me and
despite everything I must love myself
For it is my memories from which I have learned
And it is my wisdom which guides me
And it is my resolve which shall not falter.
And it is because of me, Basilisk, that I will survive."

The creature began to writhe and choke,
crying out in pain.
I allowed it to listen to everything it had to say, for I am the creature.
And when it was done, I walked to where it lay.
I scooped the thing up in my arms,
nurturing
"Come now, Basilisk.
we'll do better next time."

hey, do me a favor?

hey, do me a favor?
move a bit to the left? thanks

hey, do me a favor?
plant me in a pot near a window
and spray me with water daily
to allow my roots to spread and feed
upon the dirt

and hey, do me a favor?
when i have grown too large for the pot, can you plant me outside
in your garden
and hope with me
that the winter will not cause me to wither away
through the cold

hey, do me a favor?
close your eyes and listen
to the way that your blood rushes behind your ears
and how your breath fills your lungs
and remember the last person you
tasted

hey, do me a favor?
allow my plot to twist around your stories
and make love to the sound of your voice
reading the letters you write
to no one

hey, do me a favor?
and help me to navigate my boat
back to the dock and to feeling real again
so that i do not become beached
on nonexistence
or drown
in the water

hey, do me a favor?
and maybe remove
the dagger you left in my feathers
and help me to wash out
the blood so i
can fly again

17

do you think their souls
leaked from their bodies through the
needless bullet holes?

My Steps for Living Through a Day

Step 1
open eyes
question existence
Am I alive?
If yes, okay.
if no, shit.

Step 2
come on, legs, walk
unsteady
like a baby
stumble
it's okay, you'll get there

Step 3
Show your face to your face
look into your own eyes
step in yourself again
self-reflect
understand what is real
call out to the universe
wait for an answer
hear nothing

Step 4
open eyes
see this time
things not as blurry
see further
call out to the universe
wait for an answer
hear nothing

Step 5
Create
Create with all that you are
create with all that you have

Draw forth the rainbows within your heart
write your soul into paper
sew your spirit into the fabric
remember your mind into love
call out to the universe
wait for an answer
hear something

Step 6
Remember the way their skin felt electric on yours
the way it moved while you ran your fingers over it
the way their hair parts while you run your fingers through it
the weight of their head on your shoulder
call out to the universe
wait for an answer
feel the rest

Step 7
repeat.

the rest of my life: A Story of Unrequited Love

I've been thinking a lot lately about the difference
between surviving and existing.

A part of me is positioned at each corner of an unsteady platform.
In order to proceed, those on the platform must tilt its weight to
allow one person to get to the ladder.
Only three can make it through as one part of me is not enough.
Which part of me is going to die today?

Some of me hopes that it will be the part that loves you.
We've tried that before, it didn't go over well
but maybe if we just try one more time...
No. Not again.

That part of me wishes to spend the rest of my life with you.
It's just wondering when the rest of my life starts.
That part of me knows, it knows, it knows
that we could work, we could work, we could work
It craves it like it is stuck in a desert without water
as though your love could quench its thirst
It wishes for me to lock away my heart into a box
and I'll hold the key and you'll hold the box
until the rest of my life starts.

That part of me is so afraid of
saying the wrong thing again
that instead it says nothing
which is what I am afraid I would feel
if not for what I feel for you
I wonder if it is less that I am afraid and silent
and more that I have given you all of my words
and now I have none more to use.

One night you asked me why I'm always
looking out the window at the moon.
and I avoided the question because
the real answer was that I wanted to love you

like the moon loves the earth.
To run my hands over your surface and pull
the waves forward and back and to be with you
in the dark and maybe you'll stare deeply
into the places where I have been struck
by space rock and name the craters

And maybe that will be someday.
Maybe the rest of my life will begin.
But for now, friends will have to do.

What MapQuest Says When You Put Me In as the Destination

So, you'll want to take a left at the suit of armor.
I know that it's me under that armor but you won't
want to talk to it because if you do
it may want to try to protect you, they try to do that to everybody.

Take a right at the tree that's always on fire.
It asked god to be struck by lightning so
that all of its roots to reality could be kept warm
and she complied and it's still burning.

Keep going down this road until you get
to the heart I use to hide my scars
Don't look behind it, I don't think you'll like
what you see, and it's a really sketchy neighborhood.

You'll know you've gone too far if you
reach the wall I stare at while I'm trying to
fall asleep and upon which, if my eyes
could bite down when they close,
I would crunch my ocular teeth into and
wonder what sleep would taste like.

You'll want to pop a u-ey at my
love for the movie
Eternal Sunshine for the Spotless Mind
Feel free to pull over and watch,
though I can't guarantee you won't
arrive in the middle as it's sort of just on repeat there
because, god, I wish that movie was real.

Head east at the fork and take the
seventieth exit at the roundabout.
You'll make it to the place where
the words fly like birds in the canopies
of the trees, and if you open your
windows they'll rush in and talk to
you, I'd suggest just brushing

them off as they're not very good
conversation.

But the music notes can stay,
they have great music taste,
I made them after all.

Take exit 587 to route 3,262
you'll pass the great meteorologist
my spine, and if you're curious of
the weather you can stab it over
and over and over and over and over
again and it'll tell you if the next
snowstorm is soon. I'll be in crippling pain,
but hey, you'll know the weather.

By now you might need to stop for gas,
so if you pull off the side of the road and
burst through the concrete barrier,
you might flip a few times down the hill
but when you reach the bottom, talk to
my thirst and craving for knowledge
They'll give you a fill up in return for
intelligence and information, though
they often get attached and infatuated
to one specific subject so be sure to have
a variety of fun facts and new info.

Take a left out of the parking lot of the gas station.
and then drive straight up into the sky
and keep driving until it gets dark and the oxygen leaves
your lungs and you freeze into an icicle.
It is there you'll find my creativity.
Don't worry about the twine wrapped around it,
That's all that is keeping it held together.
Without that twine it shatters and its shards
scatter and spread all over the world
and I'd hate to have to go picking my own pieces
up again after I've fallen apart.

Level out your car and drive toward the neutron star
way off in the distance. About half way between there
and here, you'll come to the realization that it's no wonder
your heart is a muscle the size of your fist
because you were born to fight with your love,
like I try and fail often to do.

Take a left, and then three more,
and come find me. I'll be waiting.

Love Letter

Dear Storey,
I love you and
I can't imagine being
with anyone else.

I love that you
are just like a mannequin
used not for modelling matching clothes
but for mismatching body parts to feelings to thoughts

that are like dominoes
one falls into another into another into another into another
until they all fall down.

Bullets are like love
love is patient, love is kind,
love will punch holes into your being
until you are not feeling
until you are not fitting
until you are not thinking
of being anything at all.
And love will kill you.

I love that you are so good at giving your wet eyes to
all the ghosts that don't deserve them
even if you only see them in passing
through the crowds at the train station.

I love your skin
that is sometimes tree bar
and sometimes plastic
and sometimes lava erupting
from pores like volcanoes
melting, melting, melting
but not melting away.

Sincerely,

Forever and always yours,
You.

The Man Who Brings Cold Wherever He Goes

The Man Who Brings Cold
Wherever He Goes
visited me while I slept.

I can tell because I woke up numb.
As though I had been frozen in my sleep.
As though my blood was stopped in
its tracks like a car intentionally
driven into a tree or wall or life.

Curled like a pretzel of metal
Curled like a desperate cry for help
Curled like a dead, frozen forest.

The Man Who Brings Cold Wherever He Goes
visited me on the train.
I can tell because, even though
the train is still moving, I
have stopped feeling it
and now no longer progress forward.

The Man Who Brings Cold Wherever He Goes
visited me the first time I looked
in the mirror this morning.
the first time I'd felt good about myself this week.
the first time I wondered if last time would be the last time I did
nothing but hate myself.
and absolutely not the first time I wished that mirror was a liar.

The Man Who Brings Cold Wherever He Goes
visited me while I was with her.
I doubt she noticed him, most people don't,
but I could feel him pulling my strings
I could feel him stealing the words
from my mouth as I spoke them,
I could feel his hands around my neck
choking my emotions out

shaking the love I hold for her from my bones like loose change from my pockets
as though I owe him a debt
as though my love is his and only his to give.

The Man Who Brings Cold Wherever He Goes
I wish that he would stop following me around.
I wish that his icy shackles tightened around my wrists and ankles and neck would melt away.
But even the heat of this water washing over me is not enough.
Turn the dial up, not hot enough.
Turn the dial up, still not hot enough.
Turn the dial up, skin twitching and muscles writhing with every touch,
Still not enough to melt him away.

She, The Ideal Me

Life has skinned
her with its eyes.
It has left her belly-down
upon the bed and told her
that if she looks behind her,
she will be turned to salt.

Dropping the rose on
"She'll be me not."
without noticing
there is still another
petal to pull.

She is crucified upon a stake
in the city's central square.
Set below her is a burning fire
that releases stars and comets
into the sky in place of ash.

Life is like a shark,
when it gets the scent of blood,
it will want more and more
and it was no less ruthless
than when the fire licked
at her skin burning away flesh
and when it got a taste...

When the wood burned away
and the doorway below her opened
she fell and then was cradled
in the limbs of my imagination.

Where she may find herself.
Where she finds her beauty
in the thunderstorms.
Finds her power
in the earthquakes

And, if she can find her way
out, if she, the ideal me, can
become a reality, then things will
be right. I need her to find a
way out. She will find a way out.

Brass

Loss has dipped me
in molten brass.
It has melted away my
flesh and my teeth have
fallen from my mouth
leaving not but the metallic
taste of blood upon my tongue.

It has thrown me against
the ground and crumbled
the walls I built around my
self and my emotions and
my soul and it has looked
down upon me and scolded
"Rebuild them!" but I am
building sand castles
where once there was brick.
once there was brick and
I can see the tide is coming
in to wash them all away.

The waves come crashing
upon the beach wrapping me in
the foam of their crest, cooling
the metal still clinging to
my bones into a fragile shell
which envelopes me in the
paralysis of this molten prison.

Loss has left me cold and
frozen. It has burned me

down to my core, left me
not but fear and emptiness,
it has taken my ability to
speak and move and now
I am lost.

Brass II

Your husband told me
your blood looked like
paint when he found you
convulsing on the floor.

empty pill bottle clutched
in your hand like life in
your heart, breathing
desperately breathing,

desperately wanting,
desperate to set fire
to your skin just to
see something

shine in the dark again.
It takes an average of
three days for paint to dry.
It has been 13 since you

made the trip to see
your baby and my eyes
are still wet. I check every
time I think about you.

I don't think this paint
will dry anytime soon.
I know that you're not
coming back from that

and it hurts. But the
alternative to living
in this world without
you is dying in this

world without you
and I am not strong

enough
for
that.

An Untitled Collection of Short Poems

1
I wear a watch on each
wrist because I do not
know which parts of me
are real all of the time.

2
You have no messages in your mailbox.
To send a message, press 1.
For options, press 2.
For help, press 0. For help, press 0.
For help, press 0. For help, press 0.

3
Mother cries, knocked to her knees
soldier carries her daughter away
or
stands over her son's bleeding body
or
leads her family from the plane toward deportation
or
buys the poor white kid a bike.

4
Her eyes were so full of nothing
and stared at the spaces between
the lines but not at anything
before her full-of-nothing face.
She just wasn't alive anymore and
the cracks were starting to form upon
her terra cotta skin, signing the
letter D on the dotted line.

5
To thrive is so often to suffer.
To watch birds below the sunrise
is to feel the heat upon your face.
is to watch them beat the air with their wings
is to watch the clouds fade away
is to wash away the dusk, and to dream, truly dream.

6
A message to me.
You can only keep pushing if you're still alive.
Stay alive, you weak little bitch, stay alive.

7
Girl sobs, escaped from captors.
Silently crying, so bravely fighting,
a fight that should never, never, never
been started. Man scolds her,
forces her down, trumps her flight,
such great intensity, intentcity
in tent city.

8
The hard truth of this matter is
that none of these people will ever
be the same again. This has stolen from them.
No matter how strong they grow.
No matter their freedom.
No matter how high they get.
No matter how drunk they get.
There will always be something
missing because of this.

Seeds of Saturn

I knew it from the first time I saw you.
Yours would be the face that destroyed me.
Your hands, so full of fire, would be the
ones to reach into my head and pull
out my brain and wring it out like a wet towel.

There you were, from our first conversation,
lodged so deeply within that pulling you out
would fracture me in to too many bits to be
put back together again. I loved you in all the ways
I hoped to love myself someday. If my heart was
an hourglass, meeting you was what reset the sands.

I have seen sunsets and listened to waves
in conch shells. I have felt the death and rebirth
of autumn. I have felt snow pile upon my face
like tiny fairies with daggers. I have rested
through thunderstorms that rumbled like the monsters
in my head and all of it would have been
so much better if only I could have experienced
it with you. If only, if only, if only...

It was you who taught me the courage of stars,
to pierce through darkness of night even if I
am burning up inside. It was you who showed
my how to form shapes from clouds and how to
wrap myself in them and how they will protect me.
It was who made me armor of stone so
the earth would always hold me to its surface.

Every night, I take myself apart. Unsew worn skin.
Open old scars. Stay up late to pick at thoughts.
Unravel the flesh and see myself as all the mistakes
and wrongs that cost me you. Dig through muscle and
memory only to find the broken promise shaking like a
house in an earthquake, like a person crying in bed,
tears dripping into phone, as they learn that you can't

be together. It will take them long, so long, to learn that life isn't a question. It doesn't need an answer.

end.

www.ingramcontent.com/pod-product-compliance
Lightning Source LLC
Chambersburg PA
CBHW051959290426
44110CB00015B/2309